Enrichment
READING

Peggy Kaye

Dear Student,

Here is your very own *Enrichment Reading* book. The book is filled with exciting reading things to do at home. In it you will find games, contests, puzzles, riddles, information, stories, and all sorts of surprises. Best of all, you may ask your family or friends to work on the activities with you.

While you are having fun, you will be doing a lot of reading. You will also be learning how exciting reading can be.

Your friends at *Enrichment Reading* hope this book will be one of your favorite things to do. Good luck and happy reading!

AMERICAN SCHOOL PUBLISHERS

Enrichment Series Copyright © 1991 SRA/McGraw-Hill

Contents

1 My Clown

Make the clowns the same.

Draw what is missing on the second clown.

Is It the Same?

Play this with a grown-up.

Toss a penny on the Game Board.

Look at the drawing under your penny.

If you have the same drawing on your Playing Card, cross it out.

Take turns.

You win if you cross out all your drawings first.

Game Board

My Playing Card

My Grown-up's Playing Card

2 | To the Doghouse

Help the dog get home.

Draw a path from the dog to its home.

Do not cross over any lines.

It Moved

Do this with a grown-up.
Put a spoon, a fork, and a knife
on a table.
Close your eyes.
Have your grown-up move one thing.
Open your eyes.
Which thing was moved?
If you know, you may color a star.
Play 6 rounds.

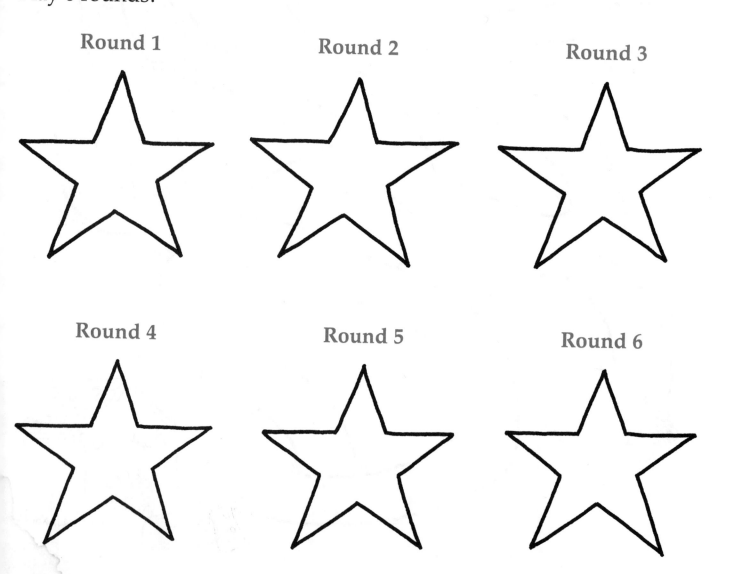

Round 1

Round 2

Round 3

Round 4

Round 5

Round 6

3 ▷ Rhyme Design

Look at the circle.

Draw lines between things
with names that rhyme.

Trace over the one done for you.

Then do the rest.

Color the shapes you made in the circle.

hat, bat, cat

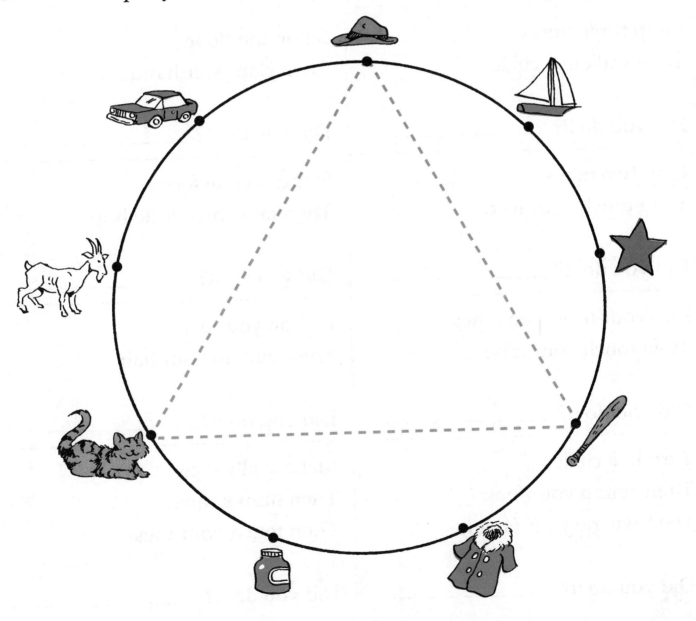

Orders

Do this with a grown-up.
Have your grown-up read each set of orders.
Then try to follow the orders exactly.
If you make a mistake, have your grown-up
read the orders again and you try again.
You have 3 chances for each set of orders.

Orders

Jump three times.
Then walk in a circle.

Did you do it? _____

Sit on the floor.
Then clap your hands.

Did you do it? _____

Clap two times.
Then touch your feet.

Did you do it? _____

Stand on one foot.
Then take three little hops.

Did you do it? _____

Rub your head two times.
Then touch your nose.

Did you do it? _____

Pull on your ear.
Then pull on your hair.

Did you do it? _____

Turn in a circle.
Then stamp your foot.
Then wiggle your fingers.

Did you do it? _____

Make a silly face.
Then hum a tune.
Then touch your toes.

Did you do it? _____

Name _____

4 ▸ Sounds, Sounds

Say the name of each picture.
Listen to the first sound you hear in the name.
Find 3 pictures with names that begin with
the same first sound.
Circle the letter under each of the 3 pictures.

y

n

e

o

k

t

s

r

Do this to find out if you are right.
  Write the 3 letters you circled.
  Write them in order here.

_____ _____ _____

If you are right, the letters spell a great word.

In My Home

Do this with a grown-up.
Look around your home.

Find something that begins with
the same sound as <u>run</u>.

Write its name. _____
Draw a picture of what you
named.

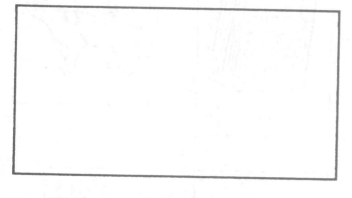

Find something that begins with
the same sound as <u>ball</u>.

Write its name. _____
Draw a picture of what you
named.

Find something that ends with
the same sound as <u>wet</u>.

Write its name. _____
Draw a picture of what you
named.

Find something that ends with
the same sound as <u>good</u>.

Write its name. _____
Draw a picture of what you
named.

5 ▶ The Farm

Look at the picture on this page.
Find 5 things with names that begin with
the same sound as <u>fall</u>.
Color them blue.

Find 5 things with names that begin with
the same sound as <u>day</u>.
Color them yellow.

Find 5 things with names that begin with
the same sound as <u>ten</u>.
Color them red.

Suitcases

Do this with a grown-up.
Help the Green family pack for a trip.
Take turns.
Draw a line from each person to things
he or she will pack.
Mom will pack things with names that begin with
the same sound as <u>mop</u>.
Dad will pack things with names that begin with
the same sound as <u>pig</u>.
Pat will pack things with names that end with
the same sound as <u>look</u>.
Bill will pack things with names that end with
the same sound as <u>well</u>.

Identifying initial and final consonant sounds

6 ▷ Tic-Tac-Toe

Look at each box in the Tic-Tac-Toe game.

Read the word and say the name

of the picture.

If the word names the picture, color the box.

When you are finished you will have tic-tac-toe.

Tic-Tac-Toe

cat	hit	fan
map	rip	can
six	tag	pin

Toss a Word

Play this game with a grown-up.

Get a penny and toss it on the game board.

Look at the letter in the space where the penny lands.

Try to use the letter to finish a word on your
Word Card.

Write the letter in the word.

Take turns.

To win, you must fill in your Word Card first.

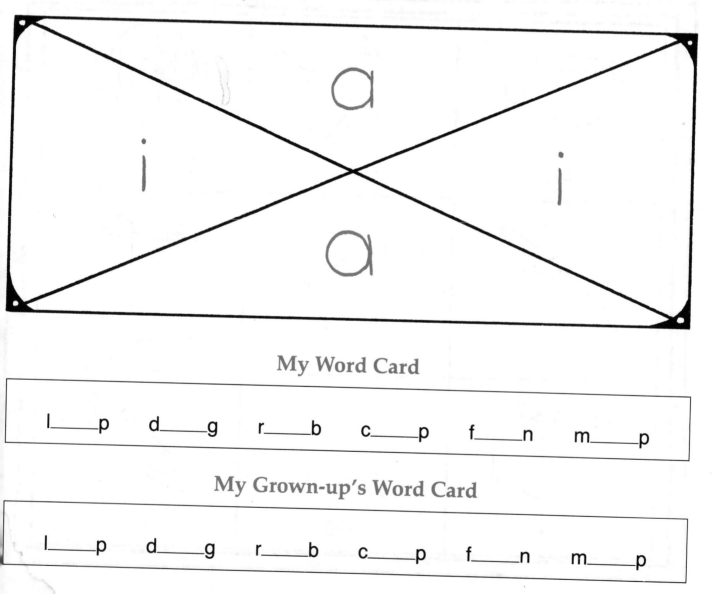

My Word Card

l___p   d___g   r___b   c___p   f___n   m___p

My Grown-up's Word Card

l___p   d___g   r___b   c___p   f___n   m___p

Name _____

7 ▷ Word Hunt

Look at each box below.

Name the picture and read the two words.

Circle the word that names the picture.

Then find the word in the Word Hunt.

The word may go across or down.

Circle the word.

The first one is done for you.

pin (pan)	map mop	cap cop
six sax	pit pot	bib bob

Word Hunt

s	i	x	m	c	p
v	k	i	p	a	o
m	o	p	a	p	t
b	i	b	n	c	a

Reading words with short *a*, *i*, and *o*   15

Make a Word

Play this game with a grown-up.
Make letter cards like these.

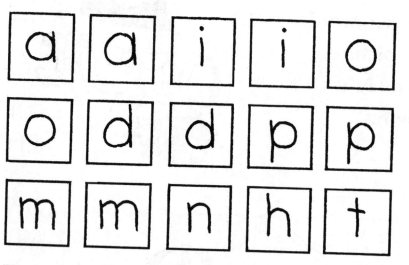

Turn over the cards.

Pick 3 cards.

Try to use the letters to make a real word.

Write the word on your Word Board.

Then turn your cards back over.

Take turns.

The first player to make 3 different words wins.

My Word Board	My Grown-up's Word Board

8 Silly Drawings

Read each sentence and do what it says.

Draw a sad pig in a big box.

Draw a pup in a tub full of mud.

Draw six big wet bugs in a cup.

Do They Sound the Same?

Play this game with a grown-up.
Make word cards like these.

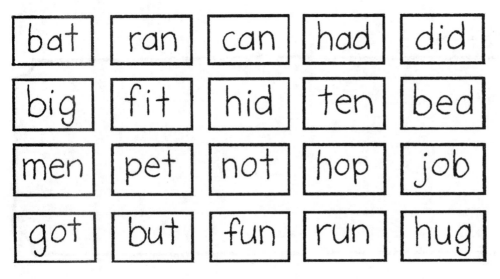

bat	ran	can	had	did
big	fit	hid	ten	bed
men	pet	not	hop	job
got	but	fun	run	hug

Turn over the cards.
Pick 2 cards.
Read the words on the cards out loud.
Listen for the vowel sounds.
If the words have the same vowel sound,
keep the cards.
If the words do not have the same vowel sound,
turn the cards back over.
Take turns.
Play until no more cards are left.
Then count your cards.

How many cards do you have? _____

How many cards does your grown-up have? _____
The player with more cards wins the game.

⑨ Word Stars

Look at the 3 word beginnings next to the first star.

Now look at the word endings in the star.

Pick a beginning for each ending.

Write it on the line.

Trace over the one done for you.

Then do the rest the same way.

bl   fl   cl

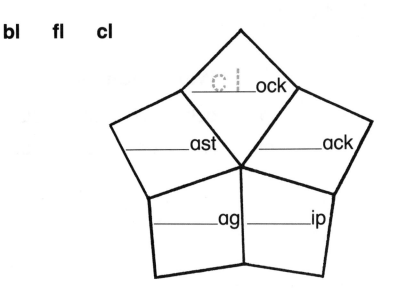

_____cl ock

_____ast   _____ack

_____ag   _____ip

sl   tr   fr

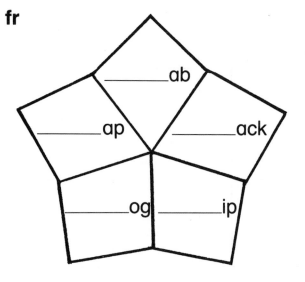

_____ab

_____ap   _____ack

_____og   _____ip

Beginnings and Endings

Play this game with a grown-up.

You will put together word beginnings and endings.

Toss a coin.

If the coin lands heads up, you may make 1 word.

If the coin lands tails up, you may make 2 words.

Write your words on your Word Card.

Take turns.

The first player to fill a Word Card wins.

I'll use **bl** and **ock**. That makes the word **block**!

Word Beginnings

bl   sl   cl   fl

gr   dr   tr   st

Word Endings

ip   ock   ap   am   ob

ab   ill   ub   ick   ess

My Word Card

My Grown-up's Word Card

Hidden Message

Look at each picture and say its name.
Listen for the beginning sound.
Color the box if the name begins with the same
sound as <u>chin</u>, <u>shoe</u>, or <u>thumb</u>.
When you finish, the colored boxes will make a word.

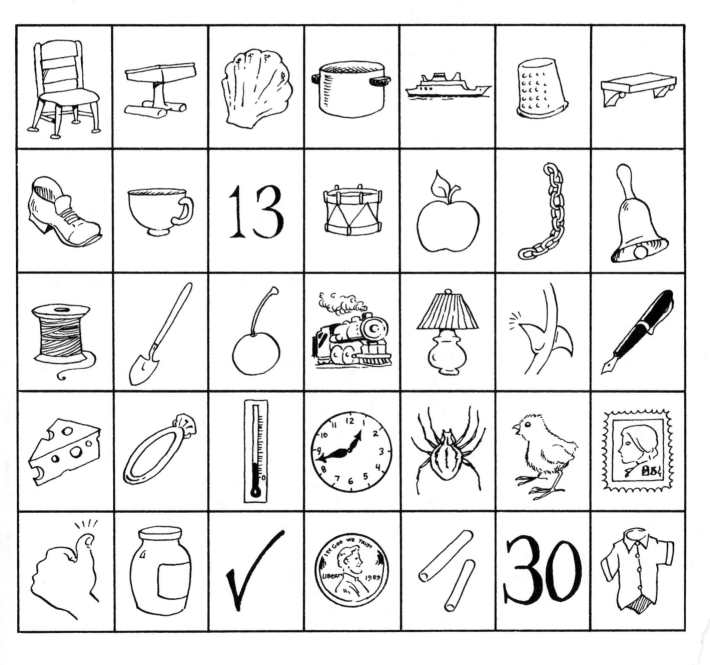

Down the Road

Play this game with a grown-up.

Make letter cards like these.

Turn over the cards.

Then get a small marker for each player.

Put the markers on GO.

Take turns picking a card.

Look at the letters on the card.

Move your marker to the next picture with a name that begins with the sound the letters stand for.

Then turn the card back over.

Play until one player lands on the last picture.

Play the game 3 or more times.

The winner is the player who lands on the last picture more often.

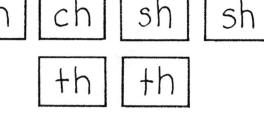

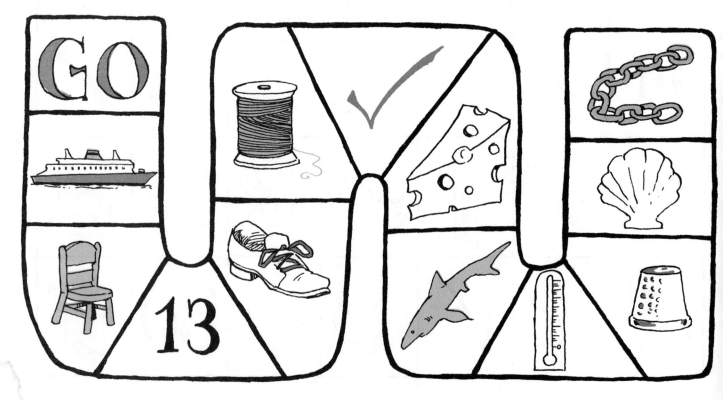

11 ▸ They Are Hiding

There are 7 things hiding in the picture.
Each thing is named in the Word Box.
Read all the words in the Word Box.
Then try to find the things in the picture.
Color the things you find.

Word Box

kite	bone
cape	cane
flute	mule
pine cone	

Word Boxes

Play this game with a grown-up.

Pick 3 boxes.

Write an **e** at the end of each word in your boxes.

Read the new words.

Score 1 point for each real word.

Keep score on a piece of paper.

Have your grown-up do the rest of the boxes.

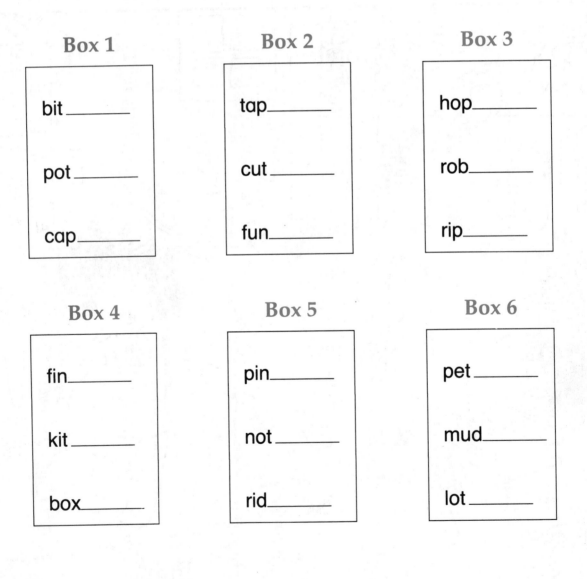

Box 1

bit _____

pot _____

cap _____

Box 2

tap _____

cut _____

fun _____

Box 3

hop _____

rob _____

rip _____

Box 4

fin _____

kit _____

box _____

Box 5

pin _____

not _____

rid _____

Box 6

pet _____

mud _____

lot _____

Who scored more points? _____

12 ❯ Who Is the Winner?

Who will be the winner?
Each child has a word card.
Add an **e** to the end of each word.
Read the new word.

The winner does not have a real word.

Who is the winner? _____

Word Wheel

Play this game with a grown-up.

Make letter cards like these.

Turn over the cards.

Pick a card.

Try to use the letter or letters to finish a word

on your Word Wheel.

Write the letter or letters that finish the word.

Then turn over the card.

Take turns.

You win if you fill in your Word Wheel first.

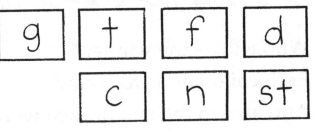

My Word Wheel   **My Grown-up's Word Wheel**

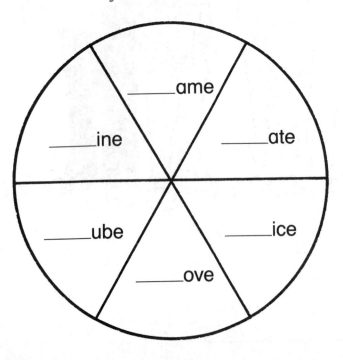

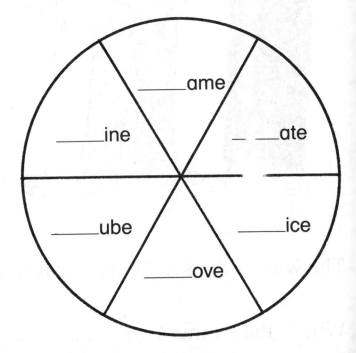

Forming words with long vowel sounds

13 ▷ Like It or Not

Read all the words in the box.
Circle every word that names something you like.
Put an **X** on every word that names something
you do not like.

rabbits	kites	parks	walking
apples	bears	bread	dolls
ball	milk	mice	playing
toys	cats	dogs	running
singing	zoos	trees	birds

Write the names of other places, foods, animals, things to do, or playthings you like.

_____

_____

_____

Write the names of other places, foods, animals, things to do, or playthings you do not like.

_____

_____

_____

Word Boxes

Play this game with a grown-up.
Make number cards like these.
Turn over the cards.
Pick a card.
Find the number on the card in the
Word List.
Read the word out loud.
If the word is in your Word Box, put an **X** on it.
If the word is not in your Word Box, turn the
card back over.
Take turns.
You win if you cross out all the words in your
Word Box first.

1	2	3	4	5
	6	7	8	9
		10	11	12

Word List

1. did	**4.** him	**7.** look	**10.** find
2. eat	**5.** could	**8.** after	**11.** who
3. was	**6.** your	**9.** put	**12.** good

My Word Box

good	was
eat	did
your	put

My Grown-up's Word Box

him	look
could	after
find	who

14 ▷ Label Me

Look at the picture.
Then read the words in the
Word Box.
Use the words in the Word Box to
label the things in the picture.
Trace over the label for <u>floor</u>.
Then do the rest.

Word Box

chair	rug	floor
toys	bed	wall
	window	

Story Words

Do this with a grown-up.

Read these 6 words.

bunny   they   from   all   party   day

Now make up a little story for your grown-up.
Use as many of the 6 words as you can.

How many of the words did you use? _____

Let your grown-up have a turn.
Your grown-up must make up a new story.

How many of the words did your grown-up use? _____

Try again with these 7 words.

down   up   water   you   more   little   ask

How many of the words did you use? _____

How many of the words did your grown-up use? _____

Now try with these 8 words.

light   name   fire   very   come   bear   girl   boy

How many of the words did you use? _____

How many of the words did your grown-up use? _____

Name _____

Zoo or Farm?

Read the story.
Each time you come to 2 words, circle the one
you want in the story.

My Story

My   mother / father   went to a   zoo / farm   .   I went too.   So did

_____

my   sister / brother   .   We went by   bus / car   .   On the way I

_____

saw a   bear / dog   .   It was   big / small   .   I said, ''I want

_____

to   help / have   it.   My   mom / dad   said I   could / could not   .

_____

What will happen now?
Draw a picture or write your idea.
Use another sheet of paper.

Word Checkers

Play this game with a grown-up.

Make 8 small red markers.

Put them on the two bottom rows of words.

Have your grown-up make 8 small blue markers.

Put them on the two top rows of words.

Then play checkers, but with one difference.

Read the word in a box before you put a marker on it.

	to		do		has		of
let		as		so		fly	
	us		for		be		old
two		now		who		way	
	get		me		by		yes
up		had		her		him	
	but		old		saw		day

16 ▶ Find the One

Read the 4 words in this box.
Three of the words go together.
Put an **X** on the word that does
not go with the other words.

cow	chicken
pig	sky

Try again with the words in these boxes.

red	blue
fish	yellow

girl	house
boy	woman

goat	chair
table	desk

ant	bee
fly	grass

Now make up your own set
of 4 words.
Make sure 3 of the words go
together.
The last word should not go
with the 3 other words.

Which Is Better?

Do this with a grown-up.

Read the words in the first box.

Put an **X** under the name of the thing you like better.

Put a ✔ under the name of the thing your grown-up likes better.

Do the rest of the boxes the same way.

apple or banana

milk or juice

lions or tigers

elephants or bears

trees or flowers

winter or summer

airplanes or trains

cars or trucks

orange or green

Make up 2 more sets of words.

Put an **X** under the names of the things you like better.

_____ or _____   _____ or _____

17 ▶ It's a Fact

How big is a baby kangaroo when it is born?
Here is how to find out.
Read each set of words.
If both words mean the same or almost
the same thing, circle the set.

cut   paint

    fast   quick

        talk   speak

            right   pen

                see   look

                    keep   save

                        sun   eat

                            always   never

How many circles did you make? _____
If you made 5 circles, a baby kangaroo can fit in a cup.
If you made 4 circles, it can fit on a thumbnail.
If you made 3 circles, it can fit in a shoe.

Fill the Balloons

Play this game with a grown-up.

Toss a coin on the game board.

Read the words in the box where the coin lands.

If the words have the same or almost the same meaning, color 2 of your balloons.

If the words have opposite meanings, color 1 balloon.

Take turns.

You win if you color all your balloons first.

happy	on	little	more
sad	off	small	less
nice	silly	up	below
mean	funny	down	under

My Balloons

My Grown-up's Balloons

Name _____

18 ▷ A Riddle

Find the mystery number.
It is the number that belongs on the next 2 lines.

The number after 8 is _____.

$5 + 4 =$ _____.

What is the mystery number? _____

Find the mystery word.
It is the word that belongs on the next 2 lines.

I gave Joe 50 _____ to buy a pencil.

The toy costs 2 dollars and 30 _____.

What is the mystery word? _____

Now here is a riddle for you.
  What is the difference between
  an old penny and a new dime?

The answer is the mystery number and the
mystery word.
Write them below to answer the riddle.

Mystery Number   **Mystery Word**

_____   _____

Lost Words

Work with a grown-up
to finish the story.
Take turns putting the lost
words back in the story.
Use words from the Word Box.

Word Box

eyes	bed	asleep
into	hug	friend
tree	sky	up
	Squirrel	

Bedtime

"It is time for bed, Little Squirrel," said Mother Squirrel.

Little Squirrel said, "I want to stay _____.

I want to climb the big oak _____. I want to

visit my _____ the frog."

"Not tonight, Little _____. The moon is high

in the _____. It is time for _____."

Mother Squirrel gave Little Squirrel a big _____.

She tucked him _____ bed. Little Squirrel closed

his _____ and fell _____.

19 ▶ Name the Pictures

Look at the pictures.
Give each picture a name.
Pick a name from the Name Box.
Write the name under the picture.

Name Box

The Picnic	The Party
A New Pup	Turtle Time

What Is Happening?

Look at this picture with a grown-up.
Talk about what is happening.

Now talk with your grown-up about these questions.

Where do you think the boy and his dad are going?

What stops them?

What do you think the boy says to his dad?

What do you think Dad says to the boy?

Give the picture a name.

My name for the picture is _____

_____.

My grown-up's name for the picture is _____

_____

Name _____

This is how to make a puppy puppet.
You need an envelope, a scissors, and a pencil.

1. Close the envelope.

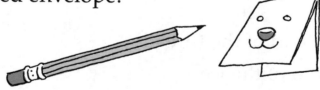

2. Cut a strip from the long side of the envelope.

 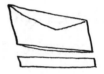

3. Fold the envelope in half.

4. Draw a puppy's eyes, nose, and mouth
on the top of the folded envelope.

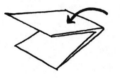 

5. Put your fingers in the top opening of the envelope.
Put your thumb in the bottom.

6. Play with your puppy puppet.

Pick Up the Ice

Do this with a grown-up.
Get an ice cube, a glass of water,
a piece of thread, and some salt.

ice cube

glass of water

piece of thread

salt

Now you will use the piece of thread
to pick up the ice cube from the
glass of water.
You will not touch the ice with
your fingers.
Just do these things and it will be
easy to lift the ice cube.

1. Put a new ice cube into the
   glass of water.

2. Dip one end of the thread
   into the water.

3. Lay the wet end of the thread
   across the top of the ice.

4. Shake salt on top of the ice cube
   and thread.

5. Let the thread stay on the top of
   the ice cube for 1 minute.
   Now slowly pull up on the thread.

21 ▶ Work Tools

Pretend you are a doctor.
Write 3 things you need for your job.

_____

_____

_____

Pretend you are a carpenter.
Write 3 things you need for your job.

_____

_____

_____

Pretend you are a teacher.
Write 3 things you need for your job.

_____

_____

_____

Fill the Lists

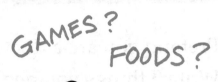

Do this with a grown-up.

Look at the Word Board.

Take turns writing words in the lists.

Choose 2 lists on each turn.

Write 1 word in each list.

Score 2 points if your word ends a list.

Keep score on a piece of paper.

The winner is the player with more points.

Word Board

Games	Colors	Animals
_____	_____	_____
_____	_____	_____
_____	_____	_____
_____	_____	_____
Foods	**Clothes**	**Numbers**
_____	_____	_____
_____	_____	_____
_____	_____	_____
_____	_____	_____

22 ▶ At the Zoo

Look at the picture.

The zoo animals are sad.

They talk to the zoo keeper.

What will the zoo keeper do now?

Write your idea.

Do not worry about spelling.

Just do your best.

_____

_____

_____

What Now?

Do this with a grown-up.
Look at the picture.

What is happening?

My grown-up thinks _____

_____.

What will happen next?

I think _____

_____.

23 ▷ Party Time

Pretend you and your best friends
want to have a party.
Plan a Best Friends Party.
Do not worry about spelling.
Just do your best.

Party Plans

Write 2 things you will do before the party.

_____

_____

Write 2 things you will do at the party.

_____

_____

Write 2 things you will do after the party.

_____

_____

The Right Order

Do this with a grown-up.

There are 4 stories on the page.

Take turns tossing a coin.

If the coin lands heads up, you read a story out loud.

If the coin lands tails up, your grown-up reads a story out loud.

Play until all the stories are read.

Story 1

Sue ate breakfast.

She woke up.

She went to school.

Story 2

Bill put on his shoes.

He put on his shirt.

He put on his socks.

Story 3

Jill liked the red flower.

She wanted the red flower.

She saw a man with flowers.

Story 4

Tom went to the store.

He got milk and apples.

He paid for the food.

Now answer this question.

Which story do you think

tells things in the right order?   **Story** _____

Turn the page upside down to check your answer.

is in the right order.

The answer is the number of the story that

How many ears do 2 rabbits have altogether? _____

24 ▸ Tim Bear

The Tim Bear is a new toy.
Look at this ad for a Tim Bear.

Tim Bear Is the Best Bear!

Tim is soft.

Tim can talk.

Tim can sing.

Tim is sold only at the Fun Time Toy Store.

Get Tim on Monday and save **$1.00**

Hi! I am Tim.

★ TIM BEAR ★

Circle the answer to each question.

Can Tim talk?	YES	NO
Can Tim walk?	YES	NO
Can you get Tim at the Super Toy Store?	YES	NO
Can you get Tim at the Fun Time Toy Store?	YES	NO
Can you get Tim on Monday?	YES	NO
Would you like to get Tim?	YES	NO

Remembering

Do this with a grown-up.

Look at the picture for as long as you want.

Then cover the picture.

Work with your grown-up to answer the questions.

How many people are in the store? _____

How many children are in the store? _____

How many dolls are on the shelf? _____

Name 2 other toys in the store. _____

_____

What toy is each child holding? _____

Name _____

Rosa and Roy have plans.
Read each set of plans.
Look for 2 things Roy or Rosa must
do before the plan can come true.
Draw a line under each thing.

The Plans

Roy wants to read a book.

1. He must pick out a book.
2. He must stand on his hands.
3. He must open up the book.

Rosa wants to cook an egg.

1. She must call her friend.
2. She must get a pan.
3. She must crack the egg.

Rosa wants to swim.

1. She must put on a swim suit.
2. She must go to the pool.
3. She must draw a picture.

Roy wants a flower garden.

1. He must get flower seeds.
2. He must eat 2 carrots.
3. He must water the seeds.

Look at the numbers next to the sentences
you underlined.
Write the numbers here.

___ + ___ + ___ + ___ + ___ + ___ + ___ + ___ = _____

Now add the numbers.
Your answer should be 16.

Why Did It Happen?

Do this with a grown-up.

Read each sentence in dark print.

Think about what it says.

Then answer the question about what happened.

Your answer may be silly or not silly.

Latoya's dog barked and barked.

What happened to make Latoya's dog bark?

I think _____

_____.

My grown-up thinks _____

_____.

David ran home as fast as he could.

What happened to make David run home?

I think _____

_____.

My grown-up thinks _____

_____.

Name _____

 Name the Person

Think of real people, storybook people, and people on TV.
Use their names when you answer these questions.

Who likes comic books?

_____

Who likes computer games?

_____

Who likes the same foods as you?

_____

Whom would you trust with a secret?

_____

Whom do you like to be with when you feel silly?

_____

Whom do you like to be with when you feel sleepy?

_____

Read this story with a grown-up.

Grandmother

Grandmother doesn't feel well. She feels sad, too. Julio and his mom are going to visit Grandmother. On the way, they want to buy four things to help Grandmother feel better and happier. What should they buy?

Write 2 things you think Julio and his mom should buy for Grandmother.

_____

_____

Have your grown-up write 2 things Julio and his mom should buy for Grandmother.

_____

_____

Name _____

Read this story about the moon.

The Moon

What makes the moon shine? The moon shines because of the sun. Light from the sun hits the moon and makes the moon glow. The moon shines all day and all night. We only see the shining moon at night when it is dark on Earth.

Now read the 2 sentences in dark print.
Draw a line under the sentence that tells what the story is mostly about.

The moon is very big.   **The sun makes the moon shine.**

April, 1950   July, 1969

Look at the date under the sentence you underlined. If you underlined the right sentence, you found the date when a person first walked on the moon.

You can check your answer.
Just turn your book upside down and read the sentence.

A person first walked on the moon in July, 1969.

What's It About?

Do this with a grown-up.

Here are 2 stories.

Each of you read your story out loud.

My Story

Marta likes her baby sister. The baby sleeps a lot. She eats a lot. She cries a lot. But when she sees Marta, she smiles a lot.

My Grown-up's Story

Don likes to cook. He can make toast. He can make soup. Once he even made a pizza. Don makes really great food. He is a very good cook.

Now look at the Game Board.

Read all the sentences out loud.

Then take turns.

Toss a penny on the Game Board.

Try to land on the sentence that tells what your story is mostly about.

You win if you land on your sentence first.

Game Board

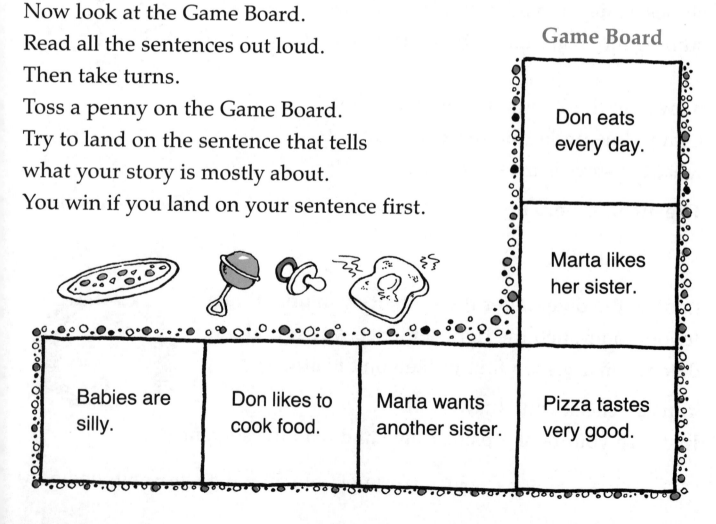

Don eats every day.

Marta likes her sister.

Babies are silly.

Don likes to cook food.

Marta wants another sister.

Pizza tastes very good.

Name _____

Read this story.

Fluff is a happy cat. She lives with a good family. Molly is 6. She loves to pet Fluff. Josh is 10. He feeds Fluff. Mom is nice, too. She brushes Fluff.

Everything is fine until the family comes home with a dog. Fluff does not want a dog.

The dog walks up to Fluff. Fluff is afraid. Fluff wants to run away. The dog licks Fluff. It feels good. Fluff licks the dog. Fluff and the dog start to play. Fluff is happy again. It is nice to have a dog for a pal. Molly, Josh, and Mom are happy, too.

Color the picture that goes with the story.

Name the Animals

Play this game with a grown-up.
Pick an animal from the Animal List.
Think about how the animal looks and acts.
Then tell your grown-up about the animal.
DO NOT tell the name of the animal.
Score 1 point if your grown-up names the animal.
Take turns.
Play 5 rounds.
Write your points on your score cards.
The winner is the player with more points.

Animal List

cat	pig	bear	lion	sheep	spider
wolf	fly	goat	horse	mouse	elephant
dog	cow	bird	tiger	hamster	squirrel

My Score Card

Round 1 _____

Round 2 _____

Round 3 _____

Round 4 _____

Round 5 _____

Total _____

My Grown-up's Score Card

Round 1 _____

Round 2 _____

Round 3 _____

Round 4 _____

Round 5 _____

Total _____

29 My Favorites

Write about your favorite things.
Do not worry about spelling. Just do your best.

My Favorite Things

My favorite time of year is _____.

I like it best because _____

_____.

My favorite holiday is _____.

I like it best because _____

_____.

My favorite game is _____.

I like it best because _____

_____.

My favorite story is _____.

I like it best because _____

_____.

Who Was First?

Do this with a grown-up.
Read each story out loud with your grown-up.
Your grown-up may help you with names.
Have your grown-up guess whom the story is about.
Draw a line under the name of your grown-up's guess.

Story 1

I made the first American flag. I used stars and stripes. Who am I?

Paul Revere

Betsy Ross

Story 2

I was the first African-American to be named a Supreme Court Judge. Who am I?

Rosa Parks

Thurgood Marshall

Story 3

I was the first First Lady of the United States. George and I never lived in the city of Washington, D.C. Who am I?

Martha Washington

Jane Adams

Story 4

I made the first light bulb. I also made the first record player and the first movie. Who am I?

Thomas A. Edison

Alexander Graham Bell

Now check your answers.

ANSWERS

Story 4 Thomas A. Edison		**Story 3** Martha Washington	
Story 2 Thurgood Marshall		**Story 1** Betsy Ross	

Name _____

Read these poems.

Polar Bear

The secret of the polar bear
Is that he wears long underwear.

                          Gail Kredenser

Oodles of Noodles

I love noodles. Give me oodles.
Make a mound up to the sun.
Noodles are my favorite foodles.
I eat noodles by the ton.

          Lucia and James L. Hymes, Jr.

HOW TO BE SERIOUS

Catch a smile

from a clown

and quickly turn it

upside down

now look

you've got

a lovely

frown.

                          Eve Merriam

Draw a picture to go with the poem you like best.

Our Poem

Finish the poem with a grown-up.
The poem may be silly or not silly.
Use words from your Word Lists.
You finish every line with ★.
Your grown-up finishes every line with ★★★.
Read the poem out loud when you are finished.

I can rhyme all the time.

My Word List					My Grown-up's Word List				
win	fin	in	grin	twin	bay	day	hay	say	play
pin	tin	thin	skin	spin	jay	pay	ray	clay	gray

★★★ Once a blue _____

★★★ all dressed in _____,

★ wanted to _____

★ at night on a _____.

★★★ It saw some _____,

★★★ it went to _____,

★ when suddenly a _____

★ said, "I want to _____."

Name _____

Read this story.

Who Will Help?

Once a hen found a wheat seed.
"Who will help me plant the seed?" she asked.

"Not I," said the duck.

"Not I," said the dog.

"Then I will do it myself," said the hen. And she did.

When the wheat was fully grown, the hen said, "Who will help cut the wheat and turn it to flour?"

"Not I," said the duck.

"Not I," said the dog.

"Then I will do it myself," said the hen. And she did.

When the flour was ready, the hen said, "Who will help me bake some bread?"

"Not I," said the duck.

"Not I," said the dog.

"Then I will do it myself," said the hen. And she did.

When the bread was done, the hen said, "Who will eat the bread?"

"I will," said the duck.

"I will," said the dog.

"No you will not!" said the hen. "I will eat it myself." And she did.

What lesson do you think the duck and the dog learned?

_____

_____

_____

After the Story Ends

Do this with a grown-up.
Read each story out loud.
Then finish the sentences about the story.

Goldilocks ran home as fast as she could go. She couldn't wait to see her mom. Goldilocks told her mom all about the 3 bears and their house in the woods. What did her mom say?

I think her mom said, "_____

_____."

My grown-up thinks her mom said, "_____

_____."

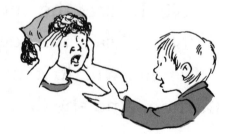

Jack cut the beanstalk. Down it came, giant and all. Jack went home with his pot of gold. He told his mother what he had done. What did his mother say?

I think his mother said, "_____

_____."

My grown-up thinks his mother said, "_____

_____."

Enrichment
READING

Grade 1
Answer Key and Teaching Suggestions

AMERICAN EDUCATION PUBLISHING

OVERVIEW

ENRICHMENT READING is designed to provide children with practice in reading and to increase their reading abilities. The program consists of six editions, one each for grades 1 through 6. The major areas of reading instruction—word skills, vocabulary, study skills, comprehension, and literary forms—are covered as appropriate at each level.

ENRICHMENT READING provides a wide range of activities that target a variety of skills in each instructional area. The program is unique because it helps children expand their skills in playful ways with games, puzzles, riddles, contests, and stories. The high-interest activities are informative and fun to do.

Home involvement is important to any child's success in school. *ENRICHMENT READING* is the ideal vehicle for fostering home involvement. Every lesson provides specific opportunities for children to work with a parent, a family member, an adult, or a friend.

AUTHORS

Peggy Kaye, the author of *ENRICHMENT READING*, is also an author of *ENRICHMENT MATH* and the author of two parent/teacher resource books, *Games for Reading* and *Games for Math.* Currently, Ms. Kaye divides her time between writing books and tutoring students in reading and math. She has also taught for ten years in New York City public and private schools.

WRITERS

Timothy J. Baehr is a writer and editor of instructional materials on the elementary, secondary, and college levels. Mr. Baehr has also authored an award-winning column on bicycling and a resource book for writers of educational materials.

Cynthia Benjamin is a writer of reading instructional materials, television scripts, and original stories. Ms. Benjamin has also tutored students in reading at the New York University Reading Institute.

Russell Ginns is a writer and editor of materials for a children's science and nature magazine. Mr. Ginn's speciality is interactive materials, including games, puzzles, and quizzes.

WHY ENRICHMENT READING?

Enrichment and parental involvement are both crucial to children's success in school, and educators recognize the important role work done at home plays in the educational process. Enrichment activities give children opportunities to practice, apply, and expand their reading skills, while encouraging them to think while they read. *ENRICHMENT READING* offers exactly this kind of opportunity. Each lesson focuses on an important reading skill and involves children in active learning. Each lesson will entertain and delight children.

When childen enjoy their lessons and are involved in the activities, they are naturally alert and receptive to learning. They understand more. They remember more. All children enjoy playing games, having contests, and solving puzzles. They like reading interesting stories, amusing stories, jokes, and riddles. Activities such as these get children involved in reading. This is why these kinds of activities form the core of *ENRICHMENT READING*.

Each lesson consists of two parts. Children complete the first part by themselves. The second part is completed together with a family member, an adult, or a friend.

ENRICHMENT READING activities do not require people at home to teach reading. Instead, the activities involve everyone in enjoyable reading games and interesting language experiences.

Published in 1995 by AMERICAN EDUCATION PUBLISHING
© 1991 SRA/McGraw-Hill

HOW TO USE HOMEWORK READING

Each *ENRICHMENT READING* workbook consists of 31 two-page lessons. Each page of a lesson is one assignment. Children complete the first page independently. They complete the second page with a family member, an adult, or a friend. The two pages of a lesson focus on the same reading skill or related skills.

Each workbook is organized into four or five units emphasizing the major areas of reading instruction appropriate to the level of the book. This means you will always have the right lesson available for the curriculum requirements of your child.

The *ENRICHMENT READING* lessons may be completed in any order. They may be used to provide practice at the same time skills are introduced at school, or they may be used to review skills at a later date.

The games and activities in *ENRICHMENT READING* are useful additions to any classroom or home reading program. Beginning on page 68 you will find additional suggestions for classroom games and activities to follow up on the *ENRICHMENT READING* lessons.

Beginning on page 70 you will find the Answer Key for *ENRICHMENT READING*. In many cases, your child's answers will vary according to his or her own thoughts, perceptions, and experiences. Always accept any reasonable answers your child gives.

For exciting activities in mathematics, try . . .

ENRICHMENT MATH

By Peggy Kaye, Carole Greenes, and Linda Schulman

Grades 1 — 6

This delightful program uses a combination of games, puzzles, and activities to extend math skills acquired in the classroom to the real-life world of children and their families. Students using *Enrichment Math* will not be bored by the usual drill-and-practice exercises—they will actually *enjoy* doing their homework!

- Stimulating home activities reinforce classroom instruction in Number Meaning, Geometry, Measurement, and Problem Solving.
- Students become involved in active learning through practical applications of the math skills they learn in class.
- Pleasurable cooperative learning experiences foster positive student feelings about math and homework.
- Interaction among students and parents or other adults is encouraged throughout the program.
- *Enrichment Math* was written by three educators who know math and how children learn.

TEACHING SUGGESTIONS
Grade 1
Optional Activities

A TIP FOR SUCCESS

Beginning readers are sure to enjoy the activities, card games, board games, puzzles, and drawing activities in Level 1 of *ENRICHMENT READING*. The directions are straightforward and easy to understand, and there are ample pictorial aids. Nevertheless, you may want to spend a few minutes explaining the lessons to your child. Feel free to play the games and do the activities before assigning them. The games and activities will prepare students for success as well as make for enjoyable reading.

Readiness

The Readiness unit contains four lessons, two covering visual skills and two covering auditory skills. To begin, children work independently to match one clown drawing to another. This activity requires children to make visual comparisons between the two clowns. Then children play a modified lotto game in which they have to discriminate between different abstract patterns. Children also play a visual memory game and complete a simple maze. Most children love solving mazes, so you may want to supplement *To the Doghouse* (page 5) by making additional mazes for your child to solve. Children may also enjoy making their own simple mazes.

The lessons covering visual skills can help you evaluate your child's visual strengths and weaknesses. Children with good visual skills are likely to do well with a reading program that emphasizes a sight vocabulary and whole language approach. Children with less developed visual skills will probably do better with a reading program that also emphasizes phonics skills.

In the first lesson covering auditory skills, children identify rhyming words. Any number of additional rhyming activities, including reciting nursery rhymes and creating nonsense rhymes, may be used to supplement this page. Next, children play an auditory memory game in which they have to remember and follow directions. In the second lesson, they match the consonant sounds heard at the beginnings and endings of words.

The lessons covering auditory skills can help you evaluate the auditory strengths and weaknesses of students. Children who have trouble recognizing rhyming sounds, remembering what they hear, or matching beginning and ending sounds of words may have some difficulty with phonics skills. If you are aware of your child's individual needs, you will be able to adjust reading instruction accordingly.

Word Skills

The Word Skills unit contains eight lessons which cover basic consonant sound and vowel sound skills. There are lessons on initial and final consonants, consonant blends, consonant digraphs, short vowels, and long vowels formed by the addition of a silent *e*.

Beginning readers will be happy to participate in the playful approach to skills practice in these lessons. You may use the lessons to help your child practice skills he or she is just learning. You may use the lessons to review skills taught previously. Since children are eager to play games, and they are willing to play the same games over and over, the games offer a perfect way to help children master skills. Once your child is familiar with the games, you will be able to assign enjoyable word skills practice all year long.

After children complete *Silly Drawings* (page 17), try this game. Make nine playing cards, each with a different short vowel word on it. Then give each child a blank tic-tac-toe board and dictate the nine words. After you say each word, have the children write it in a box on their boards. They may write the words in any boxes they choose. Now mix the cards, draw one, and read the word on it aloud. Have the children look for the word on their boards and cross it out with an X. Then draw another card and repeat the procedure. Keep playing until one child gets tic-tac-toe. This child then says, "Tic, tac, toe," and wins the game.

Vocabulary

The Vocabulary unit contains six lessons designed to help children develop strong sight vocabularies and increase their general word knowledge. Children need to develop a store of words they can read at first sight. They also need to know how to use strategies other than phonic decoding to figure out new words. In fact, the fluent reader sounds out words selectively. What's more, many of the most common used English words do not follow regular phonetic rules.

Here are some suggested activities that may be used to complement the lessons in this unit. After your child completes *Like It or Not* (page 27), try making a list of your child's likes and dislikes. Tack two large sheets of chart paper onto a wall or bulletin board. Label one chart "I Like It." Label the other chart "I Do Not Like It." Help your child write things he or she likes and dislikes on the appropriate charts. Your child may make as many entries as she or he wants. You may also want to write some of your own likes and dislikes on the charts.

After your child completes *Label Me* (page 29), try putting labels on objects at home. Have a meeting to elicit names of objects in the room. Encourage your child to name less obvious objects, such as the doorknob, light switch, and pencil sharpener. Then have your child choose four or five of the objects named and write the name of each object on a card. Let your child tape each card on the appropriate object in the room. In a few days, repeat the activity. Soon you will have a fully labeled home or room.

Word Checkers (page 32) is also designed to help children develop their sight vocabularies. You may want to keep a supply of blank checkerboards available for your use. When the time is right, fill in the boxes with a selection of important sight words. Children will like playing the game, and you will like seeing how quickly their sight vocabularies grow.

Children who use context clues to figure out new words have a big reading advantage. These children decipher words as they read. In effect, they teach themselves to read. *A Riddle* (page 37) and *Lost Words* (page 38) will help children develop this important skill. If your child likes the approach used on these pages, it is easy to create similar activities for home use. You may also extend the lesson with a game called *Buzz*. Tell a story to your child. At selected moments in the story, say "buzz" instead of a word. For example, "Once there was a *buzz* child who lived in the big, dark woods." Have your child supply an appropriate word to replace *buzz*. Accept any reasonable choice, such as *little*, *big*, *silly*, *friendly*. Then continue the story.

Comprehension

The Comprehension unit contains ten lessons, each focusing on a different aspect of comprehension. To begin, children identify the main idea of a picture. Picture clues are very important to beginning readers, and they often use illustrations to derive meaning from text. After students complete *Name the Pictures* (page 39) and *What Is Happening?* (page 40), you may want to provide them with additional practice in finding the main idea of a picture. Use interesting pictures or photographs from your picture file, or clip some pictures from old magazines. Present the pictures to the children. Ask your child questions about the pictures in the manner of *What Is Happening?* Then encourage your child to make up titles that reflect the main ideas of the pictures.

A game called *Gotcha* may be used after your child completes Lessons 20 and 23. Describe to your child how to do a simple task, such as brushing your teeth or making a sandwich, but make one or more mistakes in the description. For example, you might change the sequence: "I put the toothbrush in my mouth and then I put toothpaste on the toothbrush." or you might add an inappropriate direction: "I put the toothbrush in my mouth and then I put on my shoes." Or you might leave out some important parts of the directions: "I went into the bathroom, got a tube of toothpaste, and brushed my teeth." Each time your child catches a mistake, he or she says "Gotcha!"

To help children understand the stories they read, they should be encouraged to think about relationships of events. One way to do this is to ask children to predict outcomes based on events in stories. You may ask your child to do this as he reads by himself. Help your child record ideas on prediction cards so he may compare his predictions with what actually happens in the stories. You may also ask your child to predict outcomes when you read aloud. Pick a good moment to stop and ask, "What do you think will happen next?" When you continue reading, compare the predictions with what actually happens.

Forms of Writing

The forms of Writing unit contains three lessons in which children are exposed to nonfiction, poetry, folk tales, and fairy tales. To complement these lessons, try to read a variety of nonfiction, poetry, folk tale, and fairy tale selections to your child.

Answer Key
Grade 1–Enrichment Reading

Level 1

Page 3 *Students draw:* tassel on hat, circles on hat, hair, facial markings, circles on suit, stripes on shoes

Page 4 Results will vary.

Page 5

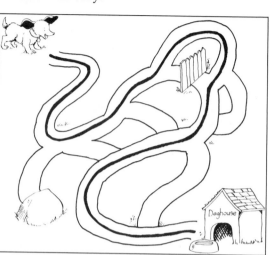

Page 6 Number of colored stars will vary.

Page 7 *Lines connect:* hat–bat–cat, boat–coat–goat, star–jar–car

Page 8 Answers will vary.

Page 9 *Circled letters:* y, e, s; yes

Page 10 Words and pictures will vary.

Page 11 *Possible blue:* farmer, fish, football, fan, fence, fox *Possible yellow:* dog, doghouse, door, dishes, duck, donkey *Possible red:* two tables, top, teapot, tomatoes, turtle

Page 12 *Mom:* mirror, map *Dad:* pajamas, pen *Pat:* bank, book *Bill:* ball, doll

Page 13 *Colored boxes:* fan, can, pin

Page 14 *Possible words:* lap, lip, dig, rib, cap, fan, fin, map

Page 15 *Circled words:* pan, mop, cap, six, pot, bib

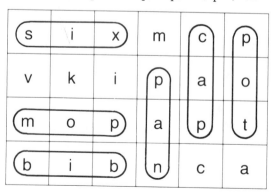

Page 16 Words will vary.

Page 17 Drawings will vary.

Page 18 Results will vary.

Page 19 *Possible words:* black, block, blast, flip, flock, flag, clip, clack, clock; slab, slack, slip, slap, track, trip, trap, frog

Page 20 *Possible words:* block, blob, bless; slip, slap, slam, slob, slab, slick; clip, clock, clap, clam, club, click; flip, flock, flap, flub, flick; grip, gram, grab, grill, grub; drip, dram, drab, drill, dress; trip, trap, tram, trill, trick, tress; stock, stab, still, stub, stick

Page 21 *Colored boxes:* chair, shoe, thread, cheese, thumb, shovel, shell, 13, cherry, thermometer, check, ship, chalk, thimble, chain, thorns, chick, 30, shelf, shirt

Page 22 Winner will vary.

Page 23 *Colored pictures:* kite, cape, flute, bone, cane, mule, pine cone

Page 24 *Box 1:* bite, cape *Box 2:* tape, cute *Box 3:* hope, robe, ripe *Box 4:* fine, kite *Box 5:* pine, note, ride *Box 6:* Pete

Page 25 *New words:* pine, cute, made, dige, bite, note; Sue

Page 26 *Possible words:* game, gate, tame, tube, fame, fate, fine, dame, date, dice, dove, dine, came, cove, cube, name, nice, nine, state, stove

Page 27 Answers will vary.

Page 28 Results will vary.

Page 29 *Labeled items:* chair, rug, floor, toys, bed, wall, window

Page 30 Stories and answers will vary.

Page 31 Circled words, pictures, and answers will vary.

Page 32 Game of checkers will vary, but students should know all the words.

Page 33 *Crossed-out words:* sky, fish, house, goat, grass; answers will vary

Page 34 Answers will vary.

Page 35 *Circled sets:* fast/quick, talk/speak, see/look, keep/save; 4

Page 36 *Words with same meanings:* little–small, silly–funny, below–under *Words with opposite meanings:* happy–sad, on–off, more–less, nice–mean, up–down; winner will vary

Page 37 *Mystery number:* 9 *Mystery word:* cents; 9 cents

Page 38 up, tree, friend; Squirrel, sky, bed; hug, into, eyes, asleep

Page 39 *Top row:* A New Pup, The Party *Bottom row:* The Picnic, Turtle Time

Page 40 Answers will vary, but should indicate the main idea of the picture.

Page 41 Puppy projects will vary.

Page 42 Students should be able to pick up the ice cube with the thread.

Page 43 Answers will vary, but should be items needed by a doctor, carpenter, and teacher.

Page 44 Words will vary, but should belong in the categories.

Page 45 Ideas will vary, but should tell what the zoo keeper might do next.

Page 46 Answers will vary, but should be related to what is shown in the picture.

Page 47 Answers will vary.

Page 48 Story 4; 4

Page 49 Yes, No, No, Yes, Yes, answers will vary

Page 50 4, 2, 3, *Possible answers:* bears, truck, robot, ball, Tim Bear or a bear

Page 51 *Book plan:* underlined sentences 1 and 3 *Swim plan:* underlined sentences 1 and 2 *Cook plan:* underlined sentences 2 and 3 *Garden plan:* underlined sentences 1 and 3; $1 + 3 + 1 + 2 + 2 + 3 + 1 + 3 = 16$

Page 52 Answers will vary.

Page 53 Names of people will vary.

Page 54 Answers will vary.

Page 55 The sun makes the moon shine.

Page 56 *My Story:* Marta likes her sister *My Grown-up's Story:* Don likes to cook food.

Page 57 Students color picture on the right.

Page 58 Results will vary.

Page 59 Answers will vary.

Page 60 *Story 1:* Betsy Ross *Story 2:* Thurgood Marshall *Story 3:* Martha Washington *Story 4:* Thomas A. Edison

Page 61 Pictures will vary.

Page 62 Poem will vary.

Page 63 Answers will vary, but should reflect the moral "You have to work for something you want."

Page 64 Answers will vary.

Also available from American Education Publishing—

MASTER SKILLS SERIES SKILL BOOKS

The Master Skills Series is not just another workbook series. These full-color workbooks were designed by experts who understand the value of reinforcing basic skills! Subjects include Reading, Math, English, Comprehension, Spelling and Writing, and Thinking Skills.

- **88 pages**   • **40 titles**   • **All-color**   • **$5.95 each**

Also Available from American Education Publishing—

BRIGHTER CHILD™ SOFTWARE

The Brighter Child™ Software series is a set of innovative programs designed to teach basic reading, phonics, and math skills in a fun and engaging way to children ages 3 - 9.

Muppet™/Brighter Child™ Software available on CD-ROM

*Same & Different	Sorting & Ordering
*Letters: Capital & Small	Thinking Skills
*Beginning Sounds: Phonics	Sound Patterns: More Phonics

also available on diskette

Brighter Child™ Software available on CD-ROM and diskette

Math Grade 1	Math Grade 2	Math Grade 3
Reading Grade 1	Reading Grade 2	Reading Grade 3

•**call (800) 542-7833 for more information**

Brighter Child™ Software Available at Stores Near You